Searchlight
BOOKS™

What's Cool
about Science?

Discover

Drones

Douglas Hustad

Lerner Publications • Minneapolis

Content Consultant: Michael S. Braasch, PhD, PE, Thomas Professor of Engineering, School of Electrical Engineering and Computer Science, Ohio University

Lerner Publications Company
A division of Lerner Publishing Group, Inc.
241 First Avenue North
Minneapolis, MN 55401 USA

For reading levels and more information, look up this title at www.lernerbooks.com.

Library of Congress Cataloging-in-Publication Data

Names: Hustad, Douglas, author.
Title: Discover drones / by Douglas Hustad.
Description: Minneapolis : Lerner Publications, [2016] | Series: Searchlight books.
    What's cool about science? | Audience: Ages 8–11. | Audience: Grades 4–6. | Includes
    bibliographical references and index.
Identifiers: LCCN 2015042712 (print) | LCCN 2015044821 (ebook) | ISBN 9781512408102
    (lb : alk. paper) | ISBN 9781512412864 (alk. paper) | ISBN 9781512410655 (eb pdf)
Subjects: LCSH: Drone aircraft—Juvenile literature.
Classification: LCC UG1242.D7 H87 2016 (print) | LCC UG1242.D7 (ebook) |
    DDC 623.74/69—dc23

LC record available at http://lccn.loc.gov/2015042712

Manufactured in the United States of America
1 – VP – 7/15/16

Contents

Chapter 1

WHAT ARE
DRONES? ... **page 4**

Chapter 2

MILITARY
DRONES ... **page 12**

Chapter 3

DRONES FOR THE PUBLIC ... **page 24**

Chapter 4

THE FUTURE OF DRONES ... **page 30**

Glossary • 38
Learn More about Drones • 39
Index • 40

WHAT ARE DRONES?

You see something flying in the sky. It looks like an airplane. But it seems too small to have a person inside. What is it? It may be a drone. A drone is an aircraft that does not have a pilot on board. Often, a person on the ground controls it. But some drones use computers to fly themselves.

Drones can fly high above the clouds. What makes drones different from normal airplanes?

Drones have many advantages over normal planes. A human pilot does not have to risk being shot down. Drones do not get tired or bored. They can fly long distances over many hours.

MILITARY DRONES CAN STAY IN THE AIR FOR DOZENS OF HOURS AT A TIME.

The military uses drones. So do companies and everyday people. Some drones have cameras in them. Farmers can use them to look at crops and livestock. Directors can use them to shoot thrilling action scenes from the air.

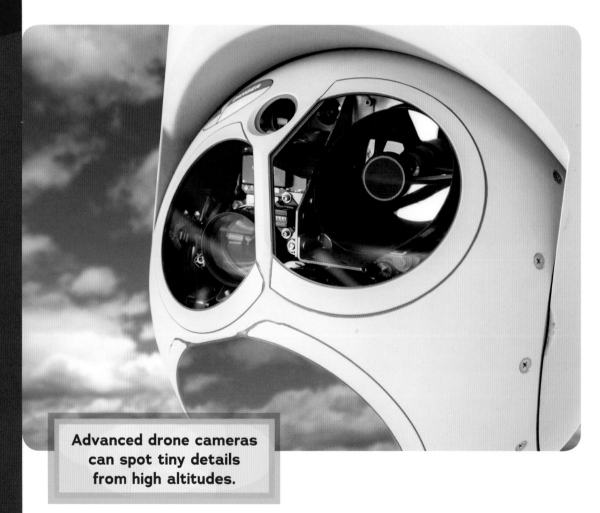

Advanced drone cameras can spot tiny details from high altitudes.

Drones' ability to see familiar surroundings from above is one reason for their popularity.

People can also use drones for fun. They can get an airborne view of their neighborhood. They can race drones through obstacle courses. They can practice their flying skills.

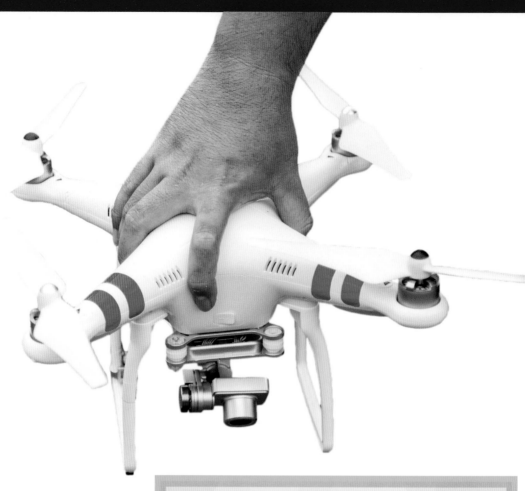

Small drones with multiple rotating blades are the cheapest and easiest to fly.

Types of Drones

Drones come in many shapes and sizes. Small types weigh just a few pounds. Some are like small helicopters. Their rotating blades push air downward. This lets them hover in place. They usually cannot fly very high or for very long.

Others look like small versions of full-sized planes. Some have propellers and broad, stiff wings. This lets them fly higher and faster.

Users often steer drones using handheld remote controls.

The biggest military drones carry enough fuel to fly thousands of miles.

Many military drones have large wings and powerful engines. These drones can weigh thousands of pounds. Some have wingspans of more than 100 feet (30.5 meters). These monsters of the sky can soar tens of thousands of feet high.

Drones are changing our world. People fly them for fun. The military uses them to carry out important missions. Companies are beginning to use them for many other purposes. The skies of tomorrow may be filled with drones of all kinds.

Some drones are small and nimble enough to dart between buildings in crowded cities.

Chapter 2

MILITARY DRONES

The US military uses drones for two kinds of missions. Drones can carry weapons to attack enemy troops. They can also take photos from high in the sky.

Military drones sometimes launch from catapults. What kinds of missions are drones used for in the US military?

Four common military drones are the MQ-1 Predator, the MQ-9 Reaper, the RQ-4 Global Hawk, and the RQ-170 Sentinel.

SOME PREDATOR DRONES HELP GUARD
FLEETS OF SHIPS.

MQ-1 Predator

Predators observe the ground from the air. They look for enemy soldiers and vehicles. They keep an eye on enemy bases. Predators use regular cameras for observing during the day. At night they switch to sensors that detect heat. This lets them see in the dark.

A Predator drone high in the sky took this image. Predators can fly as high as 25,000 feet (7,620 m).

Drone operators must keep track of lots of information at once.

The Predator can also carry two missiles and fire them at targets below. A two-person crew operates the drone from a control center. One person flies the drone. The other person controls its sensors and weapons.

THE REAPER CAN CARRY BOTH
MISSILES AND BOMBS.

MQ-9 Reaper

The Reaper is mainly used as an attack plane. It can carry up to four missiles. The drone's long range also makes it useful for keeping an eye on ground targets. Like the Predator, the Reaper is flown by two crew members back on the ground.

Reapers operate all over the world. They can be taken apart. They are loaded onto transport planes. The transport planes fly to where the drones are needed. Troops put the drones back together when they arrive. The drones then take off on their missions.

The Reaper has a wingspan of 66 feet (20.1 m).

RQ-4 Global Hawk

The Global Hawk is the largest and highest-flying US drone. It can stay in the air for more than thirty hours at a time. The Global Hawk carries no weapons. Instead, it takes incredibly sharp photos from the sky. It sends the images to the two-person ground crew. Each Global Hawk costs about $200 million.

THE GLOBAL HAWK MEASURES
47.6 FEET (14.5 M) LONG.

Firefighters in the United States have used the Global Hawk to monitor forest fires, shown here in white.

The US military introduced the latest version of the Global Hawk in 2015. The new upgrades included an advanced radar system. It helps the Global Hawk see the area around itself even more clearly. The system shoots out radio waves. The waves bounce off objects and return to a sensor. The sensor determines the location and speed of those objects.

The RQ-170 Sentinel

The Sentinel is one of the US military's most advanced drones. It was revealed to the public in 2009. The Sentinel has an unusual design. It looks like a large flying wing. Unlike most drones, it has no separate body or tail. Not much is known about the Sentinel. The government keeps most information about it secret. But experts believe it is a stealth aircraft.

The US government has not released official pictures of the Sentinel. However, experts know it has a flying-wing shape, like this experimental X-47B drone.

Stealth aircraft, such as this piloted F-117 Nighthawk, use special shapes and materials to hide from radar.

Experts think the Sentinel is designed for observation. They suspect it has high-tech cameras that provide crystal-clear views of the ground. They do not believe it carries weapons.

Controlling Drones

A satellite link lets faraway crews control drones anywhere on the planet. First, the crew gives the drone a command. They may tell it to speed up, turn, or fire a missile. This command is sent from the control center to a satellite in space. Then the satellite passes the command down to the drone. Cameras on the drone let the crews see where it is flying. This information passes through the satellite link as well.

Hundreds of satellites circle the Earth, helping people all around the world communicate.

Behind the Scenes

There are no crews aboard drones. But a huge team of people on the ground studies the pictures and video they send back. The United States Air Force has about 70,000 people assigned to examine this data.

Many US Air Force workers study the information drones beam to the ground.

Chapter 3

DRONES FOR THE PUBLIC

For many, drones are a hobby. People flying just for fun need to follow only a few basic rules. Drones must stay away from piloted aircraft. They cannot be flown close to an airport. And drones must weigh less than 55 pounds (120 kilograms). If they are larger, stricter rules apply.

The latest drones for the public are cheaper and easier than ever to fly. What rules must drone pilots follow?

These small drones are much simpler than military versions. The cheapest drones can cost less than $50. They are sold at electronics and toy stores. The most expensive cost several thousand dollars.

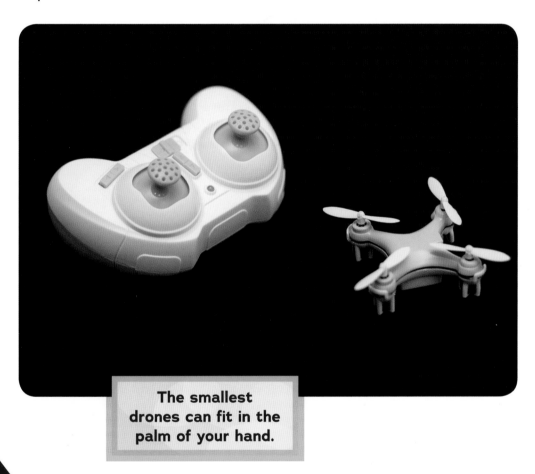

The smallest drones can fit in the palm of your hand.

One popular high-end drone is the DJI Phantom. The Phantom is a quadcopter design. This means it has four helicopter-like blades. Many drones are designed like this. Quadcopters are stable in flight. This makes it harder for them to crash. Users can attach cameras to their drones to take photos or shoot videos from the air.

The Phantom's battery can keep it flying for twenty-five minutes.

Rescued by Drones

Drones are useful for going into dangerous areas. In April 2015, a devastating earthquake hit Nepal. It caused major destruction in this South Asian nation. Rescuers struggled to find people trapped in the rubble. Drone operators were there to help. They sent drones into the sky to map the damaged areas. Cameras on the drones spotted survivors below. The drone pilots gave the location of survivors to rescue workers.

Drones watched over rescue efforts after the Nepal earthquake.

Drones have joined tractors as important pieces of equipment on modern farms.

For some people, drones are serious business. Directors can use drones with cameras to make exciting movies. Before, they needed to hire a helicopter pilot to get shots from the air. Now a drone can shoot a scene for a fraction of the price. Farmers also use drones. They may need to examine their crops or livestock. Using a drone is much faster than walking around fields on foot.

People also use drones to compete with one another. In drone races, these machines zip through courses at up to 100 miles (160 kilometers) per hour. A camera mounted at the front allows the pilot to see and steer.

Racing drones fly around obstacles and through gates at high speeds.

Chapter 4

THE FUTURE OF DRONES

Drones are already popular with the military and the public. But what does the future hold? As technology improves, engineers are developing new ways to use drones.

The drones of the future may use solar panels for electricity. What is one job future drones might do?

One of these uses is package delivery. Online shopping service Amazon.com has big goals for drones. It plans to use quadcopter drones to deliver small packages. The drones would fly from Amazon warehouses straight to customers' homes. They could carry objects weighing less than 5 pounds (2.3 kg) up to 10 miles (16 km). However, this goal is still years away. Lots of testing is needed to make sure these drones can fly through the skies safely.

Amazon showed its test drones to the public in 2013.

Drones can spot damage on power lines without putting their human operators in danger.

There are also other practical uses in the works. In California, people are testing drones for use in inspecting power lines. This work is dangerous and expensive for human workers. Drones can do it cheaper and faster.

PEOPLE WHO CONTROL DRONES FOR WORK
RECEIVE SPECIAL TRAINING.

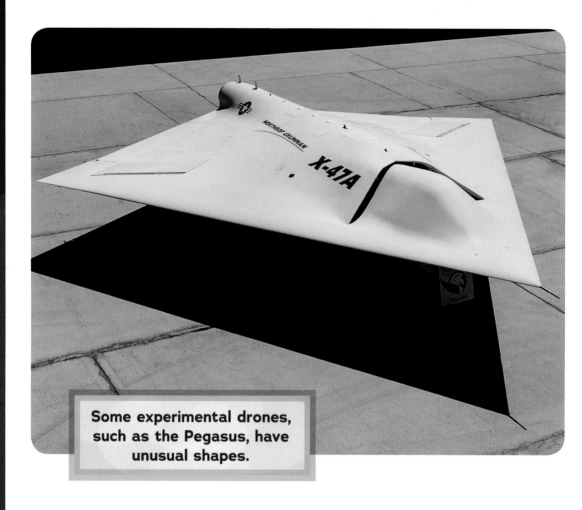

Some experimental drones, such as the Pegasus, have unusual shapes.

The future of military drones is top secret. But experts have some ideas about what might be coming. One type of drone may soar high into the sky at supersonic speeds. Another type might carry wounded soldiers away from the battlefield to a hospital.

Cutting-Edge Drones

New military drones will make even more difficult missions possible. The RQ-180 is designed to fly very high for almost twenty-four hours. And the SR-72 may be able to travel at six times the speed of sound. However, these drones are still years away from flying.

The Black Knight Transformer is designed to use eight rotors to lift wounded soldiers off the battlefield.

Drones are already doing amazing things. They can soar many miles off the ground at hundreds of miles per hour. They can use high-tech cameras to take sharp photos of objects far below.

Even drones small enough to be launched by hand are packed with incredible technology.

Our skies may someday be filled with drones doing all kinds of jobs.

Drone technology will continue to advance. Scientists and engineers will develop drones that are cheaper, more powerful, and more useful. These flying machines will help shape our future.

Glossary

military: the armed forces that protect a country

missile: a weapon that propels itself to its target before exploding

pilot: a person who flies an aircraft

propeller: a revolving set of blades on an aircraft that pushes air backward, moving the aircraft forward

remote: at a distance

satellite: an object that orbits Earth and can be used to help relay communication signals

stealth aircraft: an aircraft that is difficult to detect

supersonic: faster than the speed of sound

Learn More about Drones

Books

Henneberg, Susan. *Drones*. Costa Mesa, CA: Saddleback Educational
Publishing, 2015. Discover the many current uses of drones large
and small.

Nagelhout, Ryan. *Drones*. New York: Gareth Stevens Publishing, 2013.
Learn about the varied types of drones in use by the military.

Wood, Alix. *Drone Operator*. New York: PowerKids Press, 2014.
Go inside the life of a drone operator and see what it's like to fly
these machines.

Websites

How Drones Work

http://science.howstuffworks.com/transport/flight/modern/
drones.htm
Read facts about the history of drones and how they work.

My First Drone

http://myfirstdrone.com
Check out articles and information on buying drones and how to
fly them.

U.S. Air Force Aircraft

http://www.af.mil/AboutUs/FactSheets.aspx
Visit the official US Air Force site for fact sheets on all aircraft,
including drones.

Index

cameras, 6, 14, 21, 22, 26, 27, 28, 29, 36

delivery drones, 31

disaster areas, 27

DJI Phantom, 26

farmers, 6, 28

ground crews, 15, 16, 18, 22, 23

military drones, 6, 10–11, 12–23, 34, 35

missiles, 15, 16, 22

MQ-1 Predator, 13, 14–15

MQ-9 Reaper, 13, 16–17

quadcopters, 26, 31

racing, 7, 29

radar, 19

RQ-4 Global Hawk, 13, 18–19

RQ-170 Sentinel, 13, 20–21

rules, 24

satellites, 22

sensors, 14, 15, 19

stealth aircraft, 20

Photo Acknowledgments

The images in this book are used with the permission of: © Ninoslav Dotlic/iStock.com, p. 4; US Air Force, pp. 5, 10, 15, 16, 17, 18, 21, 23; © Feverpitched/iStock.com, p. 6; © Kletr/Shutterstock.com, p. 7; © fastfun23/Shutterstock.com, p. 8; © Peter Baxter/Shutterstock.com, p. 9; © Alexander Kolomietz/Shutterstock.com, p. 11; US Army, p. 12; US Navy, pp. 13, 19, 20, 36; © Veronique de Viguerie/Getty Images, p. 14; © 3DSculptor/iStock.com, p. 22; © Raphye Alexius/Imagesource/Glow Images, p. 24; © goldy/iStock.com, p. 25; © marekuliasz/iStock.com, p. 26; © Olivia Harris/Reuters/Corbis, p. 27; © Stefan Sauer/picture-alliance/dpa/AP Images, p. 28; © Jon Super/Rex Features via/AP Images, p. 29; © BeholdingEye/iStock.com, p. 30; © Amazon/UPI/Newscom, p. 31; © John Bazemore/AP Images, p. 32; © Gregory Bull/AP Images, p. 33; DARPA, p. 34; © Advanced Tactics/REX/AP Images, p. 35; © tiero/iStock.com, p. 37.

Front Cover: © Cpl Steve Bain ABIPP/MoD/Crown Copyright/PA Wire/AP Images.

Main body text set in Adrianna Regular 14/20.
Typeface provided by Chank.